Raupova Orasta

Bead Eye

Raupova Orasta

Bead Eye

**This book consists of events taken from the
pages of life**

JustFiction Edition

Imprint
Any brand names and product names mentioned in this book are subject to trademark, brand or patent protection and are trademarks or registered trademarks of their respective holders. The use of brand names, product names, common names, trade names, product descriptions etc. even without a particular marking in this work is in no way to be construed to mean that such names may be regarded as unrestricted in respect of trademark and brand protection legislation and could thus be used by anyone.

Cover image: www.ingimage.com

Publisher:
JustFiction! Edition
is a trademark of
Dodo Books Indian Ocean Ltd. and OmniScriptum S.R.L publishing group

120 High Road, East Finchley, London, N2 9ED, United Kingdom
Str. Armeneasca 28/1, office 1, Chisinau MD-2012, Republic of Moldova, Europe
Printed at: see last page
ISBN: 978-620-0-10516-5

RAUPOVA ORASTA

Raupova Orasta was born in 2002 in the city of Karshi. With a great love for creativity, "Golden Nash" publishing house published examples of works from the poetry collection "Ilhom Bulagok II". He was able to participate in the poetry collection "Fountains of Inspiration III" of this publishing house with poems and stories. Samples of his work were published in the poetry collection "Qalb Gavhari" organized by the professors of his institute, and he is the author of several other articles.

Raupova started her career by publishing collection of poems entitled "My Homeland Heart" in Oras.

Raupova Orasta is the winner of the international scientific and practical competition "ENTREPRENEURIAL REFORMER" organized on the scale of the Commonwealth of Independent States based on the order No. 11 of August 10, 2022 of the scientific research center "Best publication". The diploma is awarded with a certificate, a commemorative badge, a commemorative badge and a certificate.

MOTHER

I miss my chchildhood

I miss my manhood

I miss your kindness

To come to my arms

I know you are with me,

I am with you every day.

Say once, dear girl,

I miss your kindness.

Don't fight, my tongue will be coral, my youth.

You know, my heart is tender,

I miss your kindness.

There will be quarrels once a day.

Okay, let's say once a month.

You don't think about yourself.

I miss you.

I fly in the skies in the dreamy seas.

I miss your kindness,

I'm going to go far away.

I don't know if the skies are strong,

I miss your kindness.

I saw that it was life,

I knew what betrayal was.

I also gave in to fate,

I missed your kindness.

TAKE CARE OF MY PARENTS

My dreams flew away like a wind,

My prayers came like a bird.

I only asked you

I said, God save my parents.

Don't hurt him,

Let them laugh sooner or later.

Don't know why you are sad

I said, God save my parents.

Unforgettable pains,

Don't think about your sorrows.

It's enough, let it be over

I said, God save my parents.

May their faces be filled with joy,

Hearts full of love.

The pains of talking about the past,

I said, God save my parents.

You saw everything

You know, let them gather.

If you heard, howl

I said, God save my parents.

Don't make life suffer anymore,

Tokma koz Yoshin is different.

Don't talk about the exam,

I said, God save my parents.

Agree, it will be a month.

Let's be a star.

Only they light the way,

I said God save my parents.

I opened my hands and asked,

I bowed and asked.

I wish them Hajj.

I said, God save my parents.

A GIRL'S TALE

When the tulip opens in spring,

A boy entered my dream.

Stay by my side for once

I've been waiting for you to tell me for a long time.

I woke up when I said,

Then I knew it was a night.

That I will hear when I miss you,

I waited for the night.

It's been a long time, so many days

The night is far away.

When I say it's night,

I couldn't sleep for one night.

I waited a long time,

I also shouted sleep.

I close my eyes gently,

I fantasized about him.

What's in your dream

He is with another.

Mish mish these are mish mish

Well, it's a dream.

I told the dream to stop,

The grass is now in the sky.

You miss him so much

Go to that sheep when you grow up.

Marab, marab is coming,

It also includes dreams.

Gritting his teeth,

He does not say who he is.

My eyes are closed a little,

There was little sleep.

Look at midnight

My dog entered my dream.

Never stops laughing,

I'll scare you sooner or later.

If I wake up now,

I will never see it.

I opened my eyes and said thank you,

I gave my dog water and bread.

Don't come in the middle of the night

I asked for justice for my dog.

I say I've had enough

I'll say if it's morning.

That's it, I'll get up now

I give up sleep.

I don't dream anymore

I don't dream anymore

I don't want him anymore

I don't have it anymore.

I'm a fool too

I don't even remember his face.

What is this in a dream?

There is no way.

Days have passed since then,

What happened?

My heart is broken for some reason,

What happened to this heart?

I was joking at the beginning,

I dreamed at first.

I did it all at the beginning,

I mistook him for a sheep.

Needless to say,

These sheep are bad.

Even in your dreams

Stealing your dreams.

Fortunately, I saw a sheep in a dream.

I was grateful to see it.

I can't see a sheep in front of me,

I also opened my hand to prayer.

What happened in the dream

It also came to my life.

In my dream without showing my face,

He held my hand on my right

You know my dream

You heard me.

Don't mind the sheep

Remembering myself.

* * *

It will be difficult if you can't miss it,

When fire hits your heart, it burns badly.

When you are waiting for someone

The stars are speaking from the sky.

Although it is difficult, your tender heart,

Heartache seems sweet.

Even if your heart cries,

It will be a sparkling river.

Have you been deceived, my dear?

Did you fly to the sky, dear?

Believing your lies

My soul is suffering.

Don't believe in dreams, this is life

This is a world of grudges.

Taking off his mask,

This is the world I put on you.

I don't know if it hurts

I don't know if I'm waiting for you.

Don't tell your dreams,

I don't know if my heart is crying.

That's enough, stop now.

Don't stare at the heavens.

Take care of yourself

Don't believe lies.

These eyes don't cry anymore

These eyelashes do not age anymore.

Does not know why to fly

These are the dreams that make you think.

SPRING

I wanted to see it again today.

I wanted you to fix my hair.

A soft jalkalo tune,

I miss you spring.

I can't laugh when I say laugh

I can't afford to cheat.

I don't know what to do

I miss you spring.

Your winters deceived me,

My hands froze.

My heart made me cry

I miss you spring.

When will we see

I'm okay now if you ask.

Are you in my dreams now?

I miss you spring.

A bunch of flowers near my window,

This flower reminds me of you.

I miss this flower,

I miss you spring.

Do you remember the birds singing?

Let us laugh every morning.

Let the wind blow gently,

I miss you spring.

If you take out a tulip in the mountains,

My heart is broken.

I miss you too

I miss you spring.

I miss you, I miss you so much

I waited awake for your arrival.

My word to you

I miss you spring.

I WANT TO HOLD MY HAND

It's been a while,

My heart was in pain.

Tears rolled down my eyes,

I wanted to hold my hand.

My soul is suffering,

I'm looking forward to seeing you.

If it can't love, this is my heart

I wanted to hold my hand.

You don't teach to love,

To love is to be loved.

The hand turned into ice,

I wanted to hold my hand.

Don't separate us

Our epic love.

If we don't see each other, we are two

I wanted to hold my hand.

MY HEAD OF COUNTRY

(In memory of the first president of the Republic of Uzbekistan)

You shook hearts,

You destroyed the hearts with joy.

You didn't even bother to say don't go.

My countryman, tell me where you went.

You freed this country,

Hold the flag to the sky.

You missed going forward,

My countryman, tell me where you went.

You have learned wisdom from each other,

Always know what you're stressed about.

To another country with open arms,

My countryman, tell me where you went.

You didn't think of it yourself, tell me why

Always be a friend to goodness.

Look, you didn't stop for a moment,

My countryman, tell me where you went.

The moment you left, the sky cried

The sun hid for a moment.

The wind did not play a soft tune,

My countryman, tell me where you went.

Your people are crying,

He misses you and prays for you.

Holding a bunch of flowers in his hand,

It is pouring over your grave.

* * *

I'm so hard on you

Don't despise me anymore.

All my happiness in the world,

Don't forget me, man.

The sun always shines,

Don't be a dark cloud.

My path is like a star,

Smile to your heart.

You used to see

What happened to you?

Who stole your mind

Tell me what you know.

I will light your way,

It's like a moon.

You make my heart a place,

Fill my life with that.

SMILE

Laugh and forget the sorrow of the world

Laugh out loud.

For a person who loves dearly,

Smile for once.

This life has a lot of worries,

It doesn't end at all.

Looking at the sun

Smile for once.

If you hurt your loved one,

Don't worry if it hurts.

Like a song of laughter once,

Put on a smile.

There is a lot of wisdom in a smile,

A smile is a balm.

To a person who smiles,

Good people say thank you from the heart.

WHAT HAVE I DONE FOR YOU MOM?

You laugh when your heart burns

If life tests your patience, you will be patient.

I agree with everything.

You say thanks.

I'm your unloved daughter,

I am your stupid daughter who made you cry.

I am your daughter who made you sick

What have i done for you mom

When you laugh, the clouds spread from the sky,

The sun shines brightly for you.

The flower mother laughed with you,

What have I done for you mom?

I gave you a bunch of flowers,

Did I grab a cup of tea?

I don't know if I've touched you,

What have I done for you mom?

Even if the bird stopped, you didn't stop.

You did not send me grief.

You didn't run for yourself, you didn't win,

What have I done for you mom?

If there is pain, I am with you, my sweet soul,

You gave my life as my child.

My soul stuck in my throat today,

What have I done for you mom?

Come, mother, wash my guilt

My sin, repent a lot.

Hold you in my arms for once,

What have I done for you mom?

My strength is not enough for the blows of life,

Mom, I don't know how you can stand it.

I can't stand it like you, mom

What have I done for you mom?

I go home full of joy,

A bunch of flowers for you oaly.

Mother, forgive me and be your servant

What have I done for you mom?

I rarely bow down,

I don't even kiss your feet.

Put your hands on my face

What have I done for you mom?

I love you so much mom

I'm madly in love, mom.

I scattered like a star everywhere,

What have I done for you mom?

May the gates of heaven open today,

Let me give you a house today,

Mother, mother, do it for you today,

What have I done for you mom?

MY COUNTRY

My homeland is in the flower gardens where I spent my childhood,

My homeland is in the high mountains like my pride.

My country in the most incomparably bright mornings,

My Uzbeg will turn from you –

Bow down to your devotees.

The land where my grandfathers grew up,

I'm sick of pain.

The waters are my golden paradise,

My Uzbeg will turn from you –

Bow down to your devotees.

Freedom, freedom, peace,

How many of your sons won the black earth.

Your loyal guardians,

My Uzbeg will turn from you –

Bow down to your devotees.

I'M WAITING

My heart feels,

Come on know.

Always asking you,

Love torments me.

You, whom I have not seen,

Speak to my heart.

Whatever you do, be alone

You will be missed.

Warm days have come,

Spring has become a bride.

Write on the ground

He counted the lovers.

Everyone is happy,

Your flower is still thorny.

The one that has changed without getting closer,

I'm waiting for you.

Patience enough to paint nails,

Yor could not wait.

What loyalty

This is not the case.

A DREAM

My dreams fly like a swan,

Fire in my heart.

What if I don't dream

My day goes towards a big dream.

I shake my hand all the time,

Imagination leads to dreams again.

Thank you even then,

My dreams fly like a white bird.

* * *

I am a dream for someone, a dream for someone,

I am good for someone, bad for someone.

I became worthless for someone,

For someone who is a master princess.

I'm not looking for a prince, I went, my prince

The person I call my princess is a border.

I have a soul-loving value,

I have a Lord who calls me my servant.

I WANT TO GO

You are a world full of trials,

You are a world full of suffering.

Your lies will never end.

If I can pass these tests –

I wish I could go to my Lord like a flower.

I'm fed up with people's lies,

One of the worst betrayals.

Laughter on the lips, a smile in the eyes,

If I can pass these tests –

If I go to my Lord like a flower.

Don't tell me your stories

Do not think that you will be punished.

The world is the world, you know

If I could pass these tests –

If I go to my Lord like a flower.

ALMOND FLOWER

Waiting for winter to pass

You wake up your buds.

Blooming before everyone else

You spread your expressions.

Wake me up

Disturbing straw.

You say spring

Shake the branches.

Up in the morning

 I walk the gardens.

Wearing a flower on my forehead

I will write your name in my heart.

I know that spring has come in you,

You can feel the cloud crying.

Stirring the wind,

I see your leaves falling.

RAIN

Heavy rain from above,

I won't ask you in the evening.

You hurt the roof

Descending from the tarnov.

Some people like you,

With a warm blush.

Some people don't like you,

With your cold gaze.

You love spring so much,

If you let him, you will pour all the time.

Without letting the swallows fly,

Then when you say attang.

Flowers like you

The water is pouring from the head.

Give you a smile

Don't leave me.

You will not be seen in the cool summer,

When you are afraid of the sun.

They want you

You know it's hot.

Ignoring his words,

You don't go to them.

I drop it to dry it,

Sometimes you run away.

You want autumn like spring

You shed your leaves with pleasure.

Say sorry to the ground

You go forward to winter.

You can't be seen in the storm

You can relax in the mountains.

To sit on my throne,

A little aside.

I don't hate you

I really appreciate it.

Under your drops,

I totally agree.

FATHER

There was a knock on the door,

My father came.

A world brought joy,

My father came.

Take it from Olai's hand,

If you are tired, do it.

For a moment,

Take care of yourself.

I believe in tea

He caressed like a wedding.

One day he went,

I missed it.

Ulkan gave us happiness,

He gave an unbreakable throne.

It gave a flower that never fades,

He had a mountain for his children.

Daughters are smarter than each other,

A lamentation that did not say that my son is gone.

The skirt is full, grandchildren.

You are my happiness, Father.

LIFE IS A FAIRY TALE

I like watching the rainbow after the rain. Especially on rainy summer days. There are many rainy days, and today's rain left an indelible mark on my life. The drops flowing from Tarnov were both my joy and my sadness.

Every day, the neighbors were fed up with the loud knocking on the gate and started to come out to my mother. Bad habits made my father addicted to alcohol. As soon as he got drunk, he would shout on the street for hours. This time the gate was opened with shouts of "Nigor, Nigor".

My brother hugged me tightly. My mother loved my father despite his drinking since we were young.

War's quarrel was very bad this time. I don't know what happened that night, what my father said to my mother. In the morning, my mother went to work with swollen eyes.

I still remember the days when I couldn't enter the institute. Suitors never left our house. My father woke up with a severe headache. He does not remember what he did last night, there is no broken dish in his room, no knocked over cupboard. I don't think I saw him go out, my brother came to me and said:

"Dad is gone, she was crying, saying, 'Bring my sister.' Despite the fact that there are many thorns on the street, the traffic never ends. I forgot to put on my shoes as I ran out into the street in a hurry. There is no house left without knocking on the door. The only question I have when someone comes out is: "Didn't you see my dad?" If I said something else, I would cry. Thorns have entered my legs, but I don't feel pain. Then I found my father. I was happy to see my father's face. My father was always with his family. I went to him and threw the drinks on the table one by one. There was hatred in my father's eyes. He said go home in a low voice. I locked the door as soon as I entered the gate. Again, my father says that he should not leave. Dragging my hand, my father took me to his room. I was beaten in a difficult situation. Blood was flowing from my body over the white skin. I could not stand up. My eyes were closed, my father poured a bucket of water over me as if to prevent me from dying and left. My brother was rubbing my face in the ambulance, but this time I couldn't hug him.

If you give your heart to someone for the first time, you can't give it back to someone else. This happened in school days. There was a boy named Umidbek. We grew up together with him, we even went to school together. We were very close friends with him. Hope is like no other. He did not love girls. If a girl wanted to sit in front of him, he would go to another table. One of the most rowdy children of the school. From the thugs of our street. But despite this, he is very disappointed. If someone is worried, he is the first to rush to help.

Eleven years have passed since Hash Pash. It was the last day in the schoolyard. After dark everyone started the party. For some reason, Umid called into the room and closed the door. There are only two of us. Come to me and say "School is over, will you marry me now?" said. Something stirred inside me. It was as if he was eagerly waiting for these words. It was very nice. I couldn't take my eyes off him. He came close to me and held my hands tightly under my ears time seemed to stand still when you said yes. I ran out of the room. I could hear his words as I passed through every street. I did not see him when I returned. I heard from my friends that he and his family moved abroad.

After a three-hour operation, I opened my eyes in the hospital. And there was Hope. He is the owner of the hospital where I am staying. He also performed my operation. I stood up. I started trying again. I was with him in the hospital. My room was filled with flowers every day. Despite being the owner of the hospital, he was always with me. One day he came to my cravat and started talking:

- Do you remember that speech?

- What kind of speech?

- I told you!

- When?

- On the last day of school, in our room.

- I don't remember.

- That's it. He used to blush that he still had it.

- I don't remember.

- Remember. Getting married...

- Is that the case? I started to turn the sentence around because I forgot.

- It didn't come out of mine.

When I was saying, "Do you agree now?", my mother entered the room and said:

- The doctors gave permission, they said, we will go home, pack your things.

Umidbek left with a deep sigh. I didn't want to leave when I packed my things. I wish he would come to me again. When I left, he was staring out the window. At that moment, it was not his lips but his eyes that spoke...

A gentle breeze caressed my face from the taxi window. Forget everything, everything will be different. I was happy. I accepted this test of life with a smile. If it wasn't for this situation, maybe I still wouldn't have found my happiness. We had a family lunch together as if nothing had happened. Mom and dad went to their room. My brother fell asleep. It sounded as if someone threw a small stone from the window. I went to him and looked slowly. And that thug I knew was the owner of my dreams and the meaning of my life...

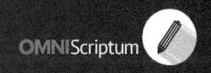

Printed by Books on Demand GmbH, Norderstedt / Germany